ROBOTICS!

Carmella Van Vleet

Illustrated by Tom Casteel

More engineering titles in the **Explore Your World!** series

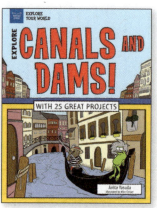
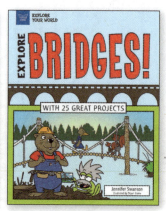

Check out more titles at www.nomadpress.net

Nomad Press
A division of Nomad Communications
10 9 8 7 6 5 4 3 2 1

This book was manufactured by Versa Press,
East Peoria, Illinois
August 2019, Job #J18-13169

ISBN Softcover: 978-1-61930-813-8
ISBN Hardcover: 978-1-61930-810-7

Educational Consultant, Marla Conn

Questions regarding the ordering of this book should be addressed to
Nomad Press
2456 Christian St.
White River Junction, VT 05001
www.nomadpress.net

Printed in the United States of America.

CONTENTS

Interested in primary sources? Look for this icon. Use a smartphone or tablet app to scan the QR code and explore more! Photos are also primary sources because a photograph takes a picture at the moment something happens.

You can find a list of URLs on the Resources page. If the QR code doesn't work, try searching the internet with the Keyword Prompts to find other helpful sources.

KEYWORD PROMPTS

robotics

ROBOTICS!

AROUND 400 BCE:
Ancient Greek inventor Archytas of Tarentum builds an automata bird.

AROUND 1500 CE:
Italian artist and inventor Leonardo da Vinci designs a self-propelled cart, now considered to be one of the earliest robots.

1986:
Honda begins working on ASIMO, an advanced humanoid that can walk, climb stairs, and recognize voice commands.

1959:
The first industrial robot, Unimate, is used in a General Motors factory.

1956:
Researcher Arthur Samuel writes a program that can play checkers.

BEGINNING IN 1615:
Japanese mechanical puppets called zashiki karakuri can serve tea.

1801:
Frenchman Joseph Jacquard invents the first programmable machine—a loom.

1948:
William Grey Walter builds Elmer, a tortoise-like robot that can sense its surroundings.

1921:
The word *robot* is first used in a play by Czech writer Karel Capek.

1822:
Inspired by Jacquard's machine, mathematician Charles Babbage designs a mechanical calculator called the Analytical Engine.

2000:
The da Vinci Surgical System is approved for use in operating rooms.

2002:
Roomba, the first popular home robotic vacuum cleaner, is sold by iRobot.

2004:
The Mars Exploration rover *Spirit* successfully lands on Mars.

2009:
Nanobots play soccer at the RoboCup competition, in a space the size of a grain of rice.

2011:
Robonaut 2 is launched into space to work alongside astronauts on the International Space Station.

2018:
The Smithsonian museums launch a pilot program using robot guides.

2017:
A robot in China performs the first dental surgery without any help from humans.

2014:
A computer passes the Turing test for the first time.

2011:
A program called Watson plays and beats two champions on the trivia gameshow *Jeopardy*.

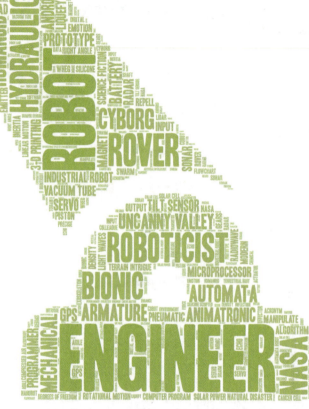

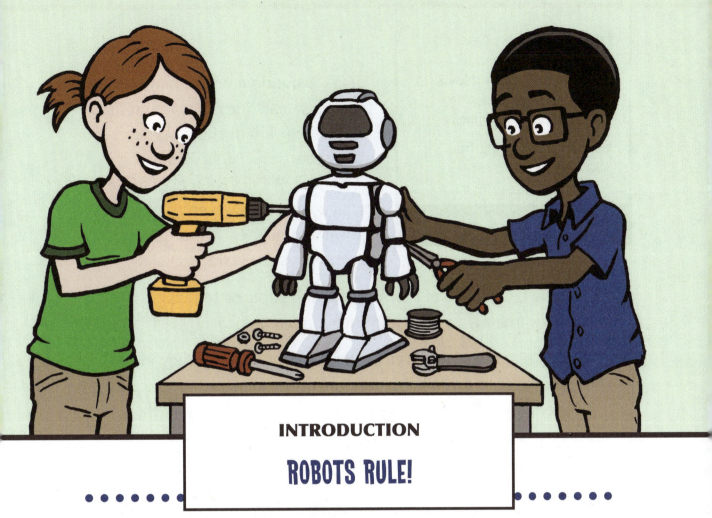

ROBOTS RULE!

Where was the last place you saw a robot? Did you read about one in a book? Or see one in a movie? Maybe you saw one in a video game. Sometimes, people think robots exist only in our imagination or as something that might be real in the future. But actually, robots are all around us right now!

A robot is a machine that can move and do tasks without help from a human. This means they can gather information from their environment, use that information to decide what to do or how to act, and then perform a task. Robots can sense, think, and act on their own.

WORDS TO KNOW

robot: a machine that can move and do tasks without help from a human.

1

Look around you right now. Are there any machines that would fit this description of robot? What about your television? Hmm . . . let's check. A television uses cables or picks up **radio waves** to play shows and movies. But it doesn't do any physical tasks.

Maybe televisions of the future will be able to tell when you're watching a movie and they'll make popcorn!

Remote-control toys aren't robots either, because they must be told what to do. What about one of those automatic vacuum cleaners? Yes! They are robots with **sensors** that allow them to sense or see their environment. They use that information to move around and do tasks, such as suck up dirt.

THIS ROBOT HELPS KEEP YOUR HOUSE CLEAN!   CREDIT: KĀRLIS DAMBRĀNS (CC BY 2.0)

DID YOU KNOW?

Many of the jobs involved in robotics are STEM jobs. STEM is an abbreviation for Science, Technology, Engineering, and Math. You might also hear it referred to as STEAM. The A in STEAM stands for Art and design.

Some people use the words *robot* and *robotics* as if they mean the same thing. But they actually have different meanings.

Robotics is the science of designing, building, controlling, and operating robots. As you can imagine, creating and operating robots can take a lot of experts from many different scientific fields. Some of these fields include engineering, math, and computer programming.

THE SENSE-THINK-ACT CYCLE

Robots use what's called the sense-think-act cycle to accomplish something.

* **SENSE:** A robot uses sensors, such as a camera, to collect information about its surroundings.

* **THINK:** A robot uses this information to decide what to do next.

* **ACT:** After a robot decides on a course of action, it carries out that action.

WHAT DO WE USE ROBOTS FOR?

On television and in movies and science fiction books, robots often resemble humans. A robot that looks like a human is called a humanoid. And they do jobs for people. Remember C-3PO? He was the fictional robot who helped Luke Skywalker in the movie, *Star Wars*.

Although most robots don't look like humans in real life, they do help us in many ways. Because they are strong and don't get tired, robots are good at helping us assemble items such as cars and other products in factories.

THESE MOVIE ROBOTS ALL LOOK DIFFERENT!

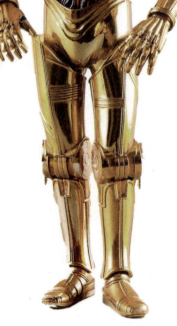

Some robots help us do jobs we don't like, don't have time for, or find boring. For example, they sweep our floors and clear our rain gutters and even clean cat litter boxes! Some robots save us time by serving drinks or food or making deliveries.

Other robots help us explore places that would be too dangerous for humans, such as deep in the ocean and far away on other planets. They can also venture into burning houses or areas in the midst of war or natural disaster and serve as helpers. And because robots can make tiny, precise movements, they can be found in many hospitals, helping doctors perform surgery, doing specialized tests, or delivering medicines to patients.

natural disaster: a natural event, such as a fire or flood, that causes great damage.

precise: exact or detailed.

solar power: energy from the sun converted to electricity.

engineer: a person who uses science, math, and creativity to design and build things.

WORDS ⓽ KNOW

STOP AND GO!

Robots are used everywhere around the world. One of these places is Kinshasa, the capital of the Democratic Republic of the Congo. Two 8-foot-tall robots direct traffic and help people safely cross the street. These robots are solar-powered and were invented by a team of female engineers led by an engineer named Isaie Therese. **You can learn more about these robots and see them in action in this video.**

KEYWORD PROMPTS

Ndiho Media Congo traffic 🔍

In *Robotics!* we'll learn more about how robots help and entertain us in our everyday lives. We'll learn about early robotics and how modern-day robots were developed. We'll explore what robots look like now and how they might look

and behave in the future. We'll also discuss how robots sense their surroundings, how they make decisions, and how they move.

Along the way, we'll design, create, play games, and experiment with robotics using items you can easily find or recycle. Let's get ready to explore!

WHAT'S A ROBOT'S FAVORITE KIND OF MUSIC? Heavy metal!

ESSENTIAL QUESTIONS

Each chapter of this book begins with an essential question to help guide your exploration of robotics. Keep the question in your mind as you read the chapter. At the end of each chapter, use your design journal to record your thoughts and answers.

? INVESTIGATE!

How many robots can you find in your home right now? Do you think that number will change in the future?

GOOD ENGINEERING PRACTICES

Every good **roboticist** keeps a design journal! In the first activity, you will make a notebook to use as a design journal. Engineers use the engineering design process to keep track of their inventions, and scientists use the scientific method to keep track of experiments.

As you read through this book and do the activities, record your observations, **data**, and designs in an engineering design worksheet or a scientific method worksheet. When doing an activity, remember that there is no right answer or right way to approach a project. Be creative and have fun!

roboticist: a scientist who studies robotics.

data: information gathered from tests or experiments.

prototype: a working model or mock-up that allows engineers to test their solution.

WORDS ⊕ KNOW

Engineering Design Worksheet
Problem: What problem are we trying to solve?
Research: Has anything been invented to help solve the problem? What can we learn?
Question: Are there any special requirements for the device? What is it supposed to do?
Brainstorm: Draw lots of designs for your device and list the materials you are using!
Prototype: Build the design you drew during brainstorming. This is your **prototype**.
Results: Test your prototype and record your observations.
Evaluate: Analyze your test results. Do you need to make adjustments? Do you need to try a different prototype?

Scientific Method Worksheet
Question: What problem are we trying to solve?
Research: What information is already known?
Hypothesis/Prediction: What do I think the answer will be?
Equipment: What supplies do I need?
Method: What steps will I follow?
Results: What happened and why?

7

PROJECT!

MAKE A ROBOT JOURNAL WITH BOOKMARK

Journals are good places to write down things you don't want to forget, such as questions you have, your ideas, or things you observe. They can also be a good place to sketch out designs. People in the STEM/STEAM fields, such as roboticists, often keep journals. You can make your own journal to keep while your read this book and learn about robotics.

1 Spread out two pieces of foil (or one long piece) on a flat surface. Make sure to put the shiny side facing down.

2 Use the ruler, pencil, and scissors to cut two pieces of poster board that are 8½ inches by 11 inches. These will be the covers of your journal.

3 Spread a thin layer of glue on the top of each piece of poster board. Before the glue dries, carefully lay the pieces of poster board on top of the foil, glue-side down. Press gently for a couple of minutes. Once the glue is set, use scissors to cut off the extra foil. Leave a little bit of foil to wrap around the edges of the poster board, about a half inch all the way around. Glue or tape it down. These will be your journal covers.

4 Place a sheet of paper on top of one of the covers. The cover should be foil-side up. Make sure the holes are on the left. Using the holes in the paper as a guide, punch matching holes in the cover. This will be your top cover.

PROJECT!

5 Lay the second cover foil-side down. Use a piece of paper and the hole punch to punch matching holes into the left side of this cover. This will be your bottom cover.

6 Sandwich several sheets of paper (the number of pages is up to you) between the two covers. Use the binder rings to secure the paper and covers together. If you don't have rings, you can use twist ties or pieces of string or yarn instead. If you do, just make sure to leave a little space when you tie them off so you can open your journal.

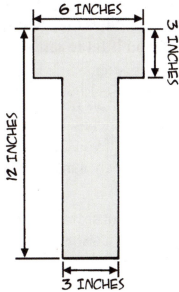

7 To make the bookmark, cut a piece of poster board into a T shape as shown.

8 Follow the same directions in Step 3 to add foil to the T-shaped piece of poster board.

9 Glue the buttons on the top of the bookmark to look like robot eyes. Place the bookmark into your journal so the whole thing will look like a robot! To keep from losing the bookmark, tape one end of a piece of string to the back of the "robot head" and tie the other to one of the binder rings.

TRY THIS! Robots do many jobs. Brainstorm a list of dangerous, boring, messy, or complicated jobs you'd like robots to do. Ask your family and friends for their ideas, too. Use your journal to record their responses.

PROJECT!

"IT'S A ROBOT!" MEMORY CARD GAME

SUPPLIES

✻ 18 blank 3-by 5-inch notecards
✻ scissors
✻ marker
✻ one or more friends

Here's a fun way to remember that robots are machines that go through the sense-think-act cycle. You'll get to test your memorization skills, too!

1 Cut six notecards in half so you have 12 pieces that are 2½ inches by 3 inches. Use the marker to write "SENSE" on one side of each card. If you can see the word through the card, use a different marker or a pencil instead!

2 Cut six more notecards in half. On these cards write "THINK." Cut the last six notecards. Write "ACT" on these cards.

TO PLAY: Shuffle all of the cards together, word side down. Lay the cards to make six rows of six cards. The players will take turns turning over three cards at a time. If they get a SENSE card, a THINK card, and an ACT card, they say, "It's a robot!" and pick up the three cards to add to their personal pile. (The cards don't have to be drawn in any particular order.) The player keeps taking a turn as long as they find a set of SENSE, THINK, ACT cards.

If the cards don't form a SENSE, THINK, ACT set, the player should turn the cards back over, facedown. The next player then tries to find their own set. Players continue taking turns until all of the sets have been found. The winner is the player with the most cards.

TIP: Pay attention when the other players draw! The better you remember where the cards are, the easier it will be for you to find the three cards you need.

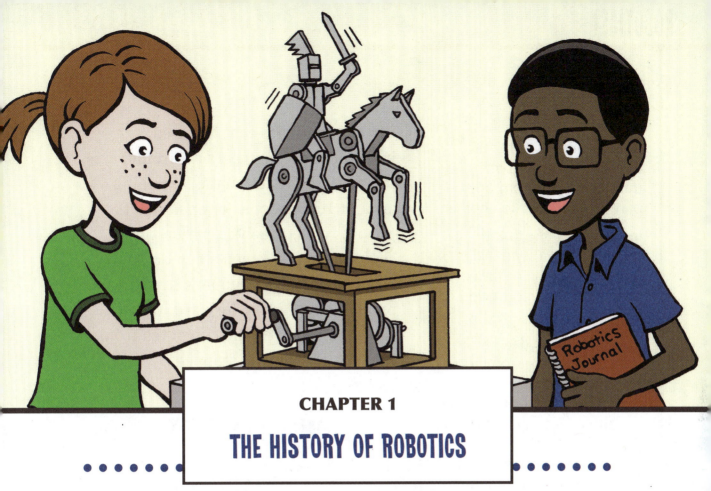

CHAPTER 1

THE HISTORY OF ROBOTICS

You might think robots are a recent invention. But people have been imagining and creating robots for hundreds of years. Early robots were called automata. They were machines or toys that moved by using things such as air, water, or gears. The computers that modern robots use weren't around then!

One of the earliest automata was a wooden bird that an ancient Greek scientist named Archytas of Tarentum (428–347 BCE) built around 350 BCE. We know the bird could flap its wings and travel a short distance along a cable or arm, but we're not certain how it was powered. Most likely it used compressed air or steam. Archytas probably used the bird to study flight.

? INVESTIGATE!

Why are people fascinated by robots?

ROBOTICS!

WORDS TO KNOW

automata: machines that can move by themselves. Singular is automaton.

gears: wheels with interlocking teeth that transfer motion from one part of a machine to another.

modern: relating to the present time, a style that is new or different, or based on the newest information or technology.

BCE: put after a date, BCE stands for Before Common Era and counts down to zero. CE stands for Common Era and counts up from zero. These non-religious terms correspond to BC and AD. This book was printed in 2019 CE.

compressed air: air that is under more pressure than the outside air.

zashiki karakuri: early Japanese automata that could serve tea.

In the centuries that followed, inventors and engineers all around the world built automata. Beginning around 1615, people in Japan made puppets called zashiki karakuri that could serve tea. When a cup of tea was placed on the puppet's tray, the puppet would move forward. When someone removed the cup of tea from the tray, the puppet stopped.

LEONARDO'S CART

Leonardo da Vinci (1452–1519) was an Italian inventor, artist, and scientist. Like many scientists, Leonardo kept journals with drawings of his inventions. Around 1478, he began sketching an idea for a self-propelled cart. It used springs and gears and could steer and brake. Because it could move on its own and be programmed to turn, roboticists consider Leonardo's cart to be an early robot.

PS Learn more about Leonardo's cart and see a model of it in action.

KEYWORD PROMPTS da Vinci inventions car

12

THE BEGINNING OF MODERN ROBOTS

The invention of computers and other technology made robots as we know them today possible. A few key developments paved the way.

First, in 1822, an English mathematician named Charles Babbage (1791–1871) designed—but never built—a mechanical calculator that he called an Analytical Engine. This machine used punch cards to solve mathematical problems.

Babbage's colleague, Ada Lovelace (1815–1852), realized that the machine could not only make calculations but could turn all kinds things—such as music and pictures—into digital form. Ada came up with an algorithm for Charles's machine. Because of this work, Ada is considered the first computer programmer.

mechanical: done by machine, not by a person.

punch card: a card with holes punched in it that gives directions to a machine or computer.

colleague: a person you work with.

digital: using numbers to express information.

algorithm: a set of steps that are followed to solve a mathematical problem or to complete a computer process.

programmer: a person who writes computer programs. Also called a coder.

WORDS ⊙ KNOW

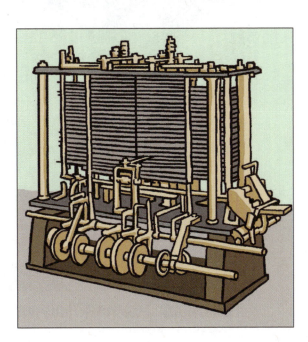

13

vacuum tube: an electronic component that looks like a light bulb. It was used as an on/off switch in early computers and other appliances.

electrical circuit: the pathway electricity follows.

transistor: a small device that acts as an on/off switch to control the flow of electricity in a computer.

WORDS TO KNOW

The invention of vacuum tubes in 1904 also played a role in the development of computers and robotics. Vacuum tubes are sealed tubes that contain no air or gas. They can be used to control electrical circuits. And computers use electrical circuits to perform tasks.

Then, in 1947, transistors made computers even faster. Transistors make it possible for robots to process information. We'll learn more about how robots think in Chapter 5.

A CODEBREAKING COMPUTER FROM 1943. COMPUTERS USED TO TAKE UP ENTIRE ROOMS!

industrial robot: a robot that works in a factory or a manufacturing setting.

WORDS ⊙ KNOW

WHAT CAME NEXT

In 1948, a scientist named William Grey Walter (1910–1977) developed the world's first robot that could sense its surroundings. This robot—named Elmer—had a cover that resembled a tortoise shell. Sensors let it "see" light and detect when it bumped into an object. Elmer used this information to change directions.

· · DID YOU KNOW? · · · · · · · · ·

Since 2002, the Robot Hall of Fame in Pittsburgh, Pennsylvania, has inducted 30 robots—both real and fictional. The last inductee was the robot from the movie *WALL-E.*

Later, William built a second, similar robot named Elsie. Elmer and Elsie helped roboticists consider how smart robots could be.

In 1954, inventor George Devol (1912–2011) came up with an idea for a robotic arm. With his partner, Joseph Engelberger (1925–2015), George turned this idea into the first industrial robot—the Unimate. In 1959, the 2,700-pound #001 prototype was installed at a General Motors plant in New Jersey. The Unimate transported pieces from an assembly line and welded them onto car bodies—a dangerous job for humans, but perfect for robots!

(PS) **Watch Elmer and Elsie navigate a room.** Are they similar to any of today's robots?

KEYWORD PROMPTS

Skitterbot Walter tortoises 🔍

At first, factory owners didn't like the idea of using robots. They didn't see how robots could be helpful. They also worried that robots would take jobs away from humans. But Joseph Engelberger worked hard to show how robots could be useful and keep humans safe from dangerous factory tasks.

Within a few years, Unimate robotic arms were performing tasks in many American car manufacturing plants. Today, most factories use robots. Because of his work, Joeseph is often called the "father of robotics."

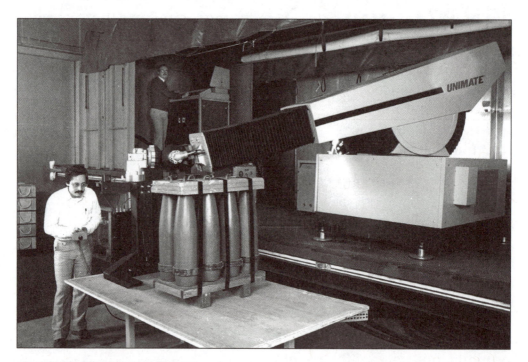

AN EARLY VERSION OF UNIMATE
CREDIT: NATIONAL INSTITUTE OF STANDARDS AND TECHNOLOGY

Watch a video about this history of the Unimate, along with interviews with George Devol and Joseph Engelberger.

KEYWORD PROMPTS

YouTube Unimate Mattfullerbridgerland

The next robotics breakthrough came in 1966, when scientists at the Stanford Research Institute in California began developing a robot called Shakey. Shakey was one of the first robots that could move and "think" for itself. For example, it could be told to find an object and knock it over.

voice recognition: the ability of a machine to recognize and respond to a human voice.

GPS: Global Positioning System, a device that determines its location on Earth using signals sent from different satellites in space.

WORDS ⊚ KNOW

Shakey had to look for the object, identify it, move to it while avoiding obstacles, and then push it over. Shakey got its name because it shook so much! The technology developed for Shakey eventually inspired other inventions, such as self-driving cars, voice recognition technology, and GPS.

·· DID YOU KNOW? ····

In 1970, *Life* magazine called Shakey the "first electronic person."

THIS AMAZON ECHO DOT IS READY TO ANSWER QUESTIONS, PLAY MUSIC, AND SOUND ALARMS. DO YOU CONSIDER THIS A TYPE OF ROBOT?

Now, robots take on many different forms and functions. They can be tiny enough to fit into your body or large enough to lift heavy machinery high above the ground. Sometimes, they look human, but more often, they don't even have a face!

We just learned about automatons that looked like people and carts and robots that looked like tortoises and arms. Who decides what a robot should look like?

We'll answer that question in the next chapter!

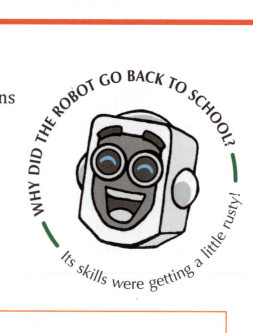

WHY DID THE ROBOT GO BACK TO SCHOOL?

Its skills were getting a little rusty!

TYPES OF ROBOTS

Throughout this book, we'll be learning about all kinds of robots and the roles they play in our lives. As you read, see if you can figure out which category the robots fall into and record your findings in your journal.

* **Domestic:** robots used to do jobs inside your home.

* **Entertainment/Sporting:** robots used for fun.

* **Social:** robots used in care or home settings.

* **Industrial:** robots found in factories and other manufacturing settings.

* **Medical:** robots used in hospitals and other health care facilities.

* **Security/Military:** robots that protect humans by doing dangerous jobs.

* **Ocean/Space:** robots that work in oceans and space.

CONSIDER AND DISCUSS

It's time to consider and discuss: Why are people fascinated by robots?

PROJECT!

SKETCH A ROBOT

SUPPLIES

✳ journal
✳ pencil, pen, or markers

As you learned earlier, Leonardo da Vinci sketched ideas for his inventions in his journals. Try doing this yourself.

1 Invite a friend to sketch a design for a robot while you do the same for your own robot.

2 Swap sketches with your friend and see if you can build a model of each other's robots using materials you find around your house. Was this hard to do?

TRY THIS! Using only your friend's sketch for clues, see if you can figure out their robot's task.

ROBOT SUPPLIES

You can use lots of things to build a robot model. Here are some things you might find around your house: old switches, old or broken toys such as dolls or model cars, LED lightbulbs, plastic tubing, pipe cleaners, cardboard or pieces of wood, foil, string or yarn, old CDs, dowels, old keyboards (make sure you ask permission before you take them apart), recycled plastic containers or tin cans, foam or poster board, empty thread spools, wire, nuts and bolts, pulleys, tape or duct tape, googly eyes, old knobs or bottle lids, empty wrapping paper or toilet paper rolls.

PROJECT!

MOVE THE KNIGHT

The cart you learned about wasn't Leonardo da Vinci's only invention. He also designed a mechanical knight that used pulleys and other systems to move. In this project, you'll make a fixed pulley system that can make a "knight's leg" move.

> **IMPORTANT:** Have an adult help with the hot glue gun and the electric drill!

1 To make the knight's leg, draw the top half of a boot on the poster board and cut it out. Glue the toilet paper roll near the back of the flat boot top. After the glue is dry, paint the leg silver. Once the paint is dry, poke two holes near the top of the leg on opposite sides.

2 Out of the shoebox lid, cut two equal-sized circles that are about a half inch bigger than the small plastic lid. Next, use the hot glue gun to glue the lid in the center of one of the cardboard pieces. Glue the second cardboard circle on top so you have something that looks like a sandwich cookie. This will be your pulley disc.

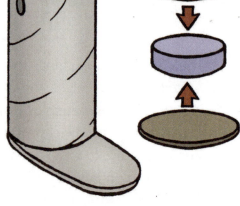

3 Have an adult help you drill a hole—just big enough for the skewer—through the middle of your pulley disc.

WORDS TO KNOW

pulley: a rope on a wheel used to lift things.

PROJECT!

4 Stand the shoebox up. Use the scissors to poke a hole in one side of the box about 2 inches from the top. You'll need enough room for your pulley disc and skewer to fit inside the box without touching any sides, so position your hole accordingly.

5 Slid one end of the skewer through the hole in the side of the box. Hold the pulley disc inside the box and slide the skewer through it and across to the other side of the box. Gently poke the skewer through the other side of the box.

6 Use scissors to poke a hole in the back of the box about half way down.

7 Cut a piece of string long enough to go through the back-of-the-box hole, up and over the pulley disc, and down to the knight leg. Run the end of the string through the holes you made in the knight leg to make a loop and tie the knot at the top.

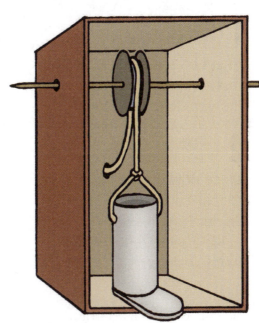

8 To lift the knight leg up, pull on the string behind the shoebox. Your pulley will do the rest!

TRY THIS! Use a fixed pulley system to move another object. Does using a pulley system make it easier?

PROJECT!

HIGH FIVE AN AUTOMATON!

Automata were often used to entertain people. You can delight your family and friends with this automaton that gives high fives.

SUPPLIES

* wire clothes hanger
* wire cutters
* pliers
* shoebox or similar sized box
* large bead
* scissors
* poster board
* plastic straws
* tape

1 Carefully unfold your hanger. Use the wire cutters to cut off the ends so you have a straight piece of wire that's about 12 inches longer than your box is wide. Use the pliers to bend one end of the wire into a handle.

2 Near the middle of the piece of wire, use the pliers to make a 90-degree bend. About 2 inches down, make a second 90-degree bend as shown.

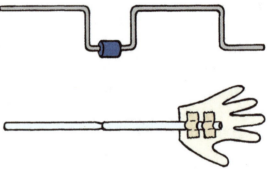

3 Slide your bead onto the open end of the wire. Next, make another 90-degree bend, going up. Make one last 90-degree bend so that you have a U-shaped dip in the middle of your wire as shown, with the bead in the middle.

4 Remove and recycle the shoebox lid. Lay your shoebox on its side, lengthwise. Use your scissors to poke holes in the middle of each side of the box. The holes should be directly across from each other.

PROJECT!

5 Keeping the part of the wire with the U bend inside the box, slide the handle through the hole in the right side of the box. You'll have to move the wire around to get it to go through. Once the handle is through the hole, maneuver the open end of the wire through the hole in the left side of the box.

6 Use a pencil to trace your opened hand onto the poster board. Cut out the hand. Crimp an end of one of the straws and insert it into the second straw to make one long straw. Use tape to attach the back of the hand to the top of the long straw.

7 Poke a hole in the top of the shoebox. Slide the long straw through the hole and rest it on the bead. The part with the hand should be above the box.

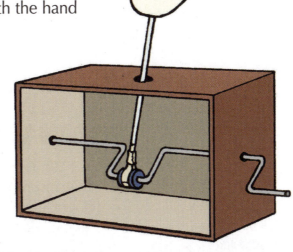

8 Use a few pieces of tape to connect the straw to the top of the bead.

9 To make your automata work, turn the handle. Your poster board hand will give you a high five!

TRY THIS! Instead of a hand, attach a cardboard bird to the top of your automaton. Can you figure out a way to get your bird's wings to flap?

PROJECT!

WRITE A ROBOT STORY

Robots can be found in many books and movies. Use your imagination to come up with your very own robot story.

1 Before you begin writing, decide who your story will be about. Is your main character a robot? What does it look like? Does it have a name? What task does it do? Maybe you can write about the robots we learned about in this chapter: Shakey, Elmer and Elsie, or Unimate. Decide what other characters will be in your story.

2 Next, start writing your story. Write what happens to your robot. What (or who) gets in your robot's way? How does your robot react? Write down what the robot and characters say to each other. Does your robot speak? Maybe it makes sounds.

3 Write what happens at the end of the story. Does your robot overcome the things that get in its way?

4 Add pictures to your story if you'd like.

• **DID YOU KNOW?** • • • • • • • • • •

In 1738, French engineer Jacques de Vaucanson (1709–1782) built "The Flute Player"—a wooden automaton that could play 12 tunes!

TRY THIS! Write your story like a comic strip. If your story is long enough, create a whole comic book.

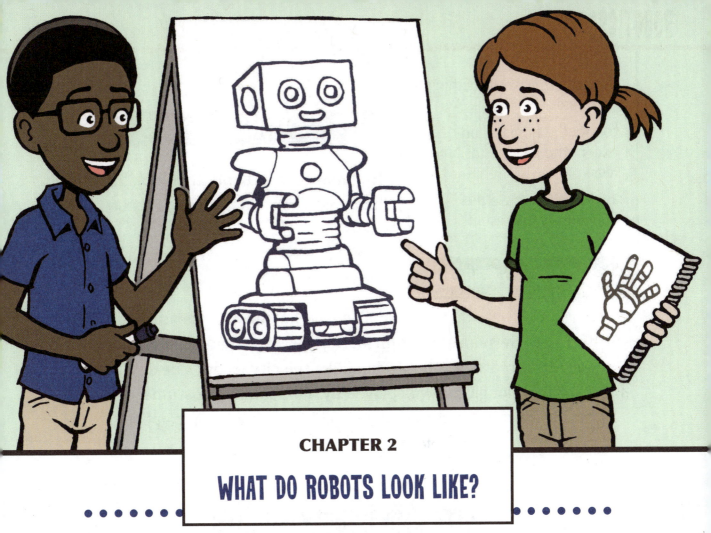

CHAPTER 2

WHAT DO ROBOTS LOOK LIKE?

If you were designing a robot to explore the ocean, how would you make it look? What materials would you use? Will the robot come across any special obstacles? What if you were designing a robot to travel to outer space? How about a robot meant to help with homework and household tasks? Would any of these robots look alike?

These are issues roboticists must think about. Robots do many different jobs, such as clean our homes, work in factories, help doctors, and disarm bombs. It's not surprising that they come in lots of shapes and sizes! Let's take a look at some of them.

? INVESTIGATE!

Why do robots often look like humans or animals?

25

HUMANOIDS

Humanoids are robots that look like humans. They usually have a **torso**, arms and legs, and a head. Some even have features that resemble a face.

The first humanoid appeared in the 1927 German silent film *Metropolis*. In the movie, a mad scientist creates a robot to look like the city leader's dead wife, Maria. Although she was played by a human in a costume, Maria the robot intrigued audiences and helped inspire people to build real humanoid robots.

CUTE AND CUDDLY ROBOTS

Social robots are used to help people feel better, teach, or entertain. They are usually cute and cuddly. Take Paro, a Japanese robot that looks like a baby seal. It has white fur and responds when you pet it. Studies have shown Paro can help reduce stress and improve relaxation levels in homes where there are elderly or sick people.

(PS) Watch Paro in action! Does this look like a pet you'd want?

KEYWORD PROMPTS

Paro video 🔍

The first humanoid robot that could move on its own was called P2. Built in 1992 by Honda, P2 could push a cart, walk, and climb stairs. In 2000, Honda used the technology developed for P2 to build ASIMO, an acronym for Advanced Step in Innovative Mobility.

ASIMO could move, walk, and climb stairs just as P2 could, but even more realistically. It weighed 119 pounds and was 47 inches tall. It could recognize objects, sounds, voices, and faces, and used two camera "eyes" to know when someone wanted to shake hands.

DID YOU KNOW?

Later ASIMO robots were slightly taller and more agile. They could also make complex decisions about their environment to help them interact better with humans.

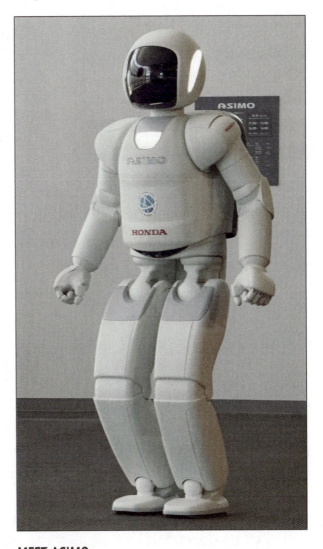

MEET ASIMO
CREDIT: CHAD KAINZ (CC BY 2.0)

ROBOTICS!

WORDS TO KNOW

mimic: to copy something.

manipulate: to handle, use, or control an object in a skillful way.

cyborg: a human or animal that is part robot.

enhance: to make greater.

bionic: a mechanical or computer-driven device that replaces or improves the normal ability of a body part.

exoskeleton: a skeleton on the outside of a body.

paralyzed: unable to move.

ICub is a humanoid roughly the size of a three-year-old child. Designed for research by RobotCub Consortium in 2004, ICub learns like children do—by exploring its environment. It has camera "eyes" that blink and move, a nose, lights for a mouth, and eyebrows to mimic human expressions. ICub can walk, crawl, and manipulate all kinds of objects. Nao, made by SoftBank Robotics, is a humanoid about the size of a baby!

CYBORGS

Cyborgs aren't robots—they're living things with enhanced abilities thanks to robotics! For example, a person missing an arm or leg might use a bionic limb. Bionic limbs operate on signals from the person's own brain and muscles. Scientists are also developing robotic exoskeletons. These metal frameworks with motorized muscles and joints allow people to move in ways they normally can't. For example, someone whose legs are paralyzed can use a robotic exoskeleton to walk.

ANDROIDS

Some humanoids look a lot like humans. These robots are called androids. Have you watched the television series *Star Trek: The Next Generation*? This show featured an android named Data. In the real world, androids aren't quite as realistic, but roboticists are close!

HRP-4C is an android also known as Miim. "She" is 62-inches tall and weighs 95 pounds. Miim has realistic "skin" on her face and hands and can mimic human facial expressions. She can also walk, sing, and dance!

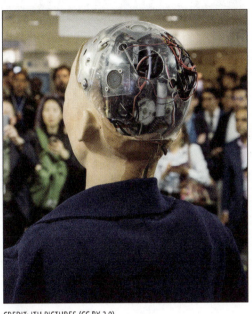

CREDIT: ITU PICTURES (CC BY 2.0)

Sophia is another well-known android. She was built by American roboticist David Hanson (1969–) and his company, Hanson Robotics. Sophia is the same size and shape as an adult female. David created a new kind of robot skin material called Frubber, short for "flesh rubber." This makes Sophia capable of amazingly realistic facial movements. She can speak, although her responses are scripted. She can also recognize human emotions and is designed to get smarter through time.

PS

Take a look at Miim laying down the moves at this website!

KEYWORD PROMPTS

Miim dance 🔍

ROBOTICS!

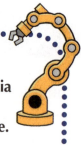

DID YOU KNOW?

Sophia was granted citizenship of Saudi Arabia in 2017, the first robot ever to have this privilege.

Roboticists hope that people will feel more comfortable working alongside robots if they look more human. But sometimes, human-looking robots don't work out too well. When a robot's appearance is real-but-not-quite-real, it enters what's called the Uncanny Valley. This is the term scientists use when a robot's appearance causes humans to feel uneasy.

ROBOTS WITH FEELINGS

Robots are machines. They don't have emotions or feelings. But they can look as if they do. Cynthia Breazeal (1967–) is a roboticist working to improve robots' facial expressions. Kismet, the robot head she made in the 1990s, was one of the first robots to recognize and respond to humans' facial expressions. Kismet can convey emotions by moving its ears, eyebrows, eyelids, jaw, lips, and head, and by changing the inflection of its voice. Human babies learn by watching and listening to their parents' exaggerated expressions and voices—what we call baby talk. Cynthia and her team used baby talk to teach Kismet to respond!

Watch Kismet respond!

KEYWORD PROMPTS

YouTube Kismet MIT

BIOMETRIC ROBOTS

Robots don't always look like humans, of course. Sometimes, they look like tools or vehicles. And sometimes, robots look like animals. Biometric robots look or behave like things in nature.

BigDog is 240-pound, four-legged robot created in 2005. BigDog is used by the military to help carry heavy equipment. It can travel over rough terrain and even across ice. Because it has legs with joints like real animals do, it can keep its balance if it's knocked into.

WORDS TO KNOW

swarm: a group of identical robots designed to work together as a team.

nanobot: a microscopic robot.

microscopic: something so small it can be seen only using a microscope.

cancer cell: a normal cell in the body that changes and grows out of control.

GhostSwimmer is another military biometric robot. This underwater robot is 5 feet long, weighs almost 100 pounds, and has fins. It looks like a shark! Though GhostSwimmer is smaller than a typical shark, it can move like one. It uses its robotic tail to change directions.

Roboticists are also developing robot **swarms** that behave like bees and other insects. BionicAnts are robots that look like—guess what—ants! About the size of a man's palm, BionicAnts work together. They mimic how real ants coordinate and communicate in nature.

DID YOU KNOW?

Pleurobot looks and crawls like a salamander. It can swim like a real salamander, too. Developers hope Pleurobot can be used for search-and-rescue missions.

NANOBOTS

Nanobots are **microscopic** robots. They are smaller than a speck of dust! One day, nanobots might be able to help fight **cancer cells** or other diseases by working together in a swarm inside a body. In 2009, nanobots played soccer in a space the size of a grain of rice at the RoboCup competition. Teams had to push a "nanoball" across the field, move around an obstacle course, and get the nanoballs across the goal.

WHAT'S IT MADE OF?

The materials used to make a robot often depend on the robot's job. You might not build a robot out of cloth if you are going to send it to the bottom of the ocean, right?

Remember BigDog? This robot must travel over difficult terrain and be strong enough to carry heavy loads. Its frame is made of sturdy metal. GhostSwimmer works in the ocean, so its body must be able to stand up to salt water. And since GhostSwimmer uses a tail to swim, the material must be flexible.

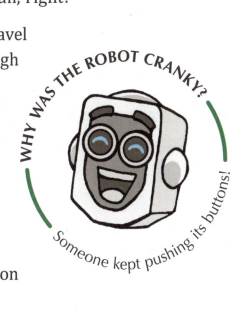

WHY WAS THE ROBOT CRANKY?

Someone kept pushing its buttons!

Sometimes, roboticists invent their own materials. For example, David Hanson invented Frubber for Sophia's face.

·· DID YOU KNOW? ·········

Furby and Elmo Live are considered animatronic toys. Movies such as *Jurassic Park*, *Jaws*, and *ET* used animatronics.

A lighter robot can be made more quickly and more cheaply. For this reason, many roboticists use silicone or plastic. Roboticists also use 3-D printing because it allows them to make robot parts easily and less expensively than other traditional methods. Making custom bionic limbs is another great use of 3-D printing.

Metal and plastics are not the only materials roboticists use. Some roboticists use everyday materials such as Lego blocks, Tinkertoys, cardboard, wood, or even rubber bicycle tires! This is especially true when they're in the early stages of designing robots and want to test things out by creating prototypes.

? CONSIDER AND DISCUSS

It's time to consider and discuss: Why do robots often look like humans or animals?

Roboticists not only think about how a robot looks, they also have to think about how a robot does its tasks. We'll take a look at how robots interact with their environments in the next chapter!

PROJECT!

MAKE SOME ROBOT SKIN

Not all robots have human-like skin such as Sophia and Miim. Although this recipe won't be the same as Frubber or other high-tech materials, it will still look cool!

1 Empty the two gelatin packets into the microwave-safe container. Add 4 tablespoons water.

2 Add 4 tablespoons of glycerin. Mix these first three ingredients together. The mixture will look like a gel.

3 Add a few drops of your paint or liquid foundation makeup into the mix and stir together.

4 Place your mixture into the microwave on high for 10 to 30 seconds until the mixture liquefies.

5 Carefully pour the mixture into the shallow pan and cool for 30 minutes in the refrigerator. It doesn't matter if the mixture fills the pan; you just need a place for the skin to cool. After it's cooled, carefully peel the skin off.

SUPPLIES

* 2 packets of unflavored gelatin
* measuring spoons
* water
* glycerin (found at many pharmacies)
* mixing spoon
* acrylic paint or liquid foundation makeup
* microwave
* shallow baking pan

TRY THIS! How does this robot skin look and what does it feel like? Record your thoughts in your journal.

WORDS to KNOW

liquefy: to turn into a liquid.

35

PROJECT!

ADD FEATURES TO ROBOT SKIN

Details help make robots look more real. Using this skin wax, experiment with creating various textures and features. This material won't dry out, so you can reuse it.

SUPPLIES

* small plastic container with lid
* measuring spoons
* flour
* petroleum jelly
* acrylic paint or liquid foundation makeup (optional)
* tools to create details (toothbrush, material, coins, toothpicks, butter knife, nail, old paint brush)

1 Scoop 6 tablespoons of flour into the container.

2 Add 2 tablespoons petroleum jelly. Add paint or makeup if you want to add some color. The wax will be beige if you don't color it.

3 Use the measuring spoon or your fingers to mix the ingredients together until they form a soft, dough-like ball. If the mixture is sticky, add a little more flour. If it's lumpy or crumbly, add petroleum jelly.

4 Lay the lid of your plastic container flat. Press your skin wax into it. You can also mold your wax around a small ball to make a robot head if you'd like.

5 Create skin texture by experimenting with various tools or items. Can you figure out how to make wrinkles, moles, dimples? How about scars?

TRY THIS! This project uses petroleum jelly. Petroleum is an oily liquid found in nature that burns easily. Research other things we use it for.

PROJECT!

MAKE A MODEL OF ROBONAUT 2

Robonaut 2, or R2, was a humanoid that worked on the International Space Station from 2011 to 2018. Its job was to be an extra pair of hands and eyes to help the astronauts do various jobs. Create a model of R2's torso with hands that can hold things.

IMPORTANT: Ask an adult to help with the hot glue gun and cutting the pieces of PVC pipe.

1 In a well-ventilated area, lay newspapers out and spray paint the milk jug. If you place the jug upside down on a bottle, you can spray paint the whole jug at once. Next, spray paint the shoebox. Let both pieces dry.

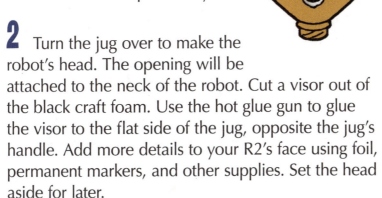

2 Turn the jug over to make the robot's head. The opening will be attached to the neck of the robot. Cut a visor out of the black craft foam. Use the hot glue gun to glue the visor to the flat side of the jug, opposite the jug's handle. Add more details to your R2's face using foil, permanent markers, and other supplies. Set the head aside for later.

WORDS ⊕ KNOW

International Space Station: a massive space station orbiting Earth where astronauts live, conduct experiments, and study space.

PROJECT CONTINUES ON NEXT PAGE . . .

SUPPLIES

* newspaper
* gallon milk jug
* copper-colored spray paint
* shoebox
* scissors
* sheet of black craft foam
* hot glue gun
* art supplies
* 5 feet of 1-inch PVC pipe
* piece of wooden board 12 inches by 12 inches
* PVC flange for 1-inch pipe (with screws)
* white long-sleeved T-shirt, adult size medium
* 1-inch PVC cross joint
* screwdriver
* pillow filling
* pair of white gloves, found at most craft stores
* poster board
* 16-gauge brass wire
* duct tape

3 Ask an adult to help you cut the PVC pipe into four pieces: one piece that is 18 inches long and three pieces that are 12 inches long. Note that you may have to adjust the length of the pieces later, depending on the shirt's size.

4 In the center of your board, attach the flange. Insert the 18-inch piece of PVC pipe and then attach the cross joint at the top of the 18-inch pipe.

5 Insert the 12-inch pieces of pipe into each of the joint openings. When you're done, you should have something that looks like a lowercase T.

6 Place the shirt over your T-shaped structure so it's "wearing" it. Part of the pipe will be sticking up through the shirt's neck. Hot glue the bottom of the shirt to the board. Stuff the shirt with pillow filling. Don't worry about closing the ends of the sleeves for now.

7 Place the robot's head on top of the PVC pipe. Use duct tape to attach it to the pipe and keep it from wobbling. Next, use the hot glue to close the top of the shirt around the pipe.

PROJECT!

8 To make the robot's hands, trace each glove onto the poster board and cut it out. Now, cut pieces of brass wire long enough to go down the middle of each finger and thumb. Use the duct tape to tape the wires securely to the poster board.

9 Carefully stuff each glove with its poster board/wire hand. Add stuffing to the gloves if you'd like.

10 Use the hot glue gun to attach the gloves to the end of the T-shirt sleeves.

11 Attach the shoebox to the back of the robot using the hot glue gun or duct tape. This represents your robot's power source.

TRY THIS! In 2014, NASA added legs to Robonaut 2. Can you think of a way to add legs to your model?

Learn more about R2 and see it in action here.

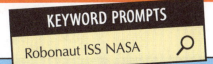

KEYWORD PROMPTS

Robonaut ISS NASA

PROJECT!

ROBOT CHARITY

Humans prefer robots that look friendly. But can a friendly looking robot inspire someone to give more money to charity? Here's a simple experiment to test this question.

IMPORTANT: Ask an adult for help with the utility knife.

1 Cover your workspace with newspaper and paint both cans the same color. Let dry.

2 About 3 inches from the top of each can, use the utility knife to carefully cut an opening that is ½-inch wide by 2-inches long.

3 Next, glue the googly eyes above the slot on one of the cans. Push the thumbtacks into each side of this can for your robot's ears. Use the utility knife to poke small holes in the sides of the can and insert the pipe cleaners to make arms. Now, you have one plain can and one friendly can!

A ROBOT'S PLEA

Do people treat robots with kindness? In 2018, German scientists conducted an experiment. They had volunteers interact with a friendly robot named Nao. Next, the scientist asked the volunteers to turn Nao off. Nao was programmed to say, "No! Please do not switch me off! I'm scared that it will not brighten up again!" to half of the volunteers. He didn't say anything to the other half. The results showed that most people who heard Nao's plea took twice as long to turn it off.

4 Decide on a charity you'd like to give to. Use the marker and notecard to create signs for each can. For example, if you choose a pet rescue organization, you could write: Coins for Cats.

5 Set up the banks near each other in the same place. This might be your home, classroom, or a nearby business that's agreed to help you. Always ask permission.

6 In your journal, start a scientific method worksheet and write a hypothesis about which bank will get more donations.

7 After a set amount of time (maybe a week), collect the cans and see which one has more money in it. Was your hypothesis correct?

TRY THIS! Donate the money you collect to your charity of choice! Share your results with them.

SHOW EMOTIONS

How does your face show your emotions? Find out with this simple experiment that you can do with a friend.

1 Ask a friend to make expressions to show various emotions, such as fear, sadness, surprise, happiness, anger, and boredom.

2 Pay attention to how your friend's face changes each time. Sketch what happens to their eyes, eyebrows, and mouth in your journal.

3 See if you can copy your friend's expression.

TRY THIS! Take turns making faces and see if the other person can guess which emotion you're trying to show.

ROBOTS WITH EMOTIONS?

Some robots can respond to a human's emotions, but robots having true emotions themselves is probably way off in the future. We can program a robot to look "happy" when it does its job, but that's not a true emotion. True emotions involve physical responses, such as racing hearts or goosebumps, and are based on our own experiences. For instance, one person might hate spiders and another person might love them.

WORDS TO KNOW

emotion: a strong feeling about something or somebody.

42

CHAPTER 3

HOW DO ROBOTS DO THINGS?

• • • • • • • • • • • • • • • • • • • •

Robots move around their environments in many different ways. If they're humanoid, such as ASIMO or Miim, they use legs. Military robots often use a tread system. Some tiny robots vibrate to travel around. Many other robots use wheels.

• •

Think about all the robots you have seen in real life, watched in movies, or read about in books. How do they move? And how does their purpose in the world influence how they move?

? **INVESTIGATE!**

What kinds of jobs will robots do in the future?

No matter how they move, all robots have three things in common. One, they have a power source. Two, that power source activates an **actuator** to make the robot move. And three, robots act upon their environment using **effectors**. Let's take a closer look at these parts: the power source, actuator, and effector.

POWER SOURCES

Industrial robots typically stay in one place. They are often very large and plugged into an electrical outlet. Some robots that move around are also powered through electricity from an outlet. Most robots, however, get their power from **batteries**. These batteries can be small or quite large.

nuclear power: power produced by splitting atoms, the tiniest pieces of matter.

solar cell: a device that converts light energy into electricity.

NASA: National Aeronautics and Space Administration, the U.S. organization in charge of space exploration.

rover: a vehicle used to explore the surface of a planet or a moon.

terrestrial body: a planet or moon that has a solid surface.

WORDS TO KNOW

Some places don't have convenient electrical outlets or a way to recharge a battery. Remember Wall-E? He used solar power. Solar cells use the sun's light to create electricity. Many robotic lawn mowers use solar power. NASA uses solar power for many of the rovers it sends to other planets, including Mars.

These rovers explore the surface of a terrestrial body and send information back to scientists on Earth. *Sojourner*, the first rover NASA sent to Mars, had a flat, square solar panel that helped charge the vehicle's batteries. Later rovers had solar "wings" that allowed them to collect more of the sun's energy.

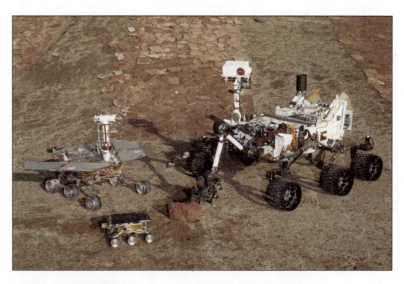

THREE GENERATIONS OF MARS ROVERS. *SOJOURNER* IS IN THE FRONT. CREDIT: NASA/JPL-CALTECH

hydraulic: describes a system that pushes and pulls objects using tubes filled with fluid.

force: a push or pull applied to an object.

piston: a short, solid piece of metal that moves up and down inside a cylinder to create motion.

pneumatic: describes a system that pushes and pulls objects using tubes filled with air or other gases.

solenoid: an electromagnetic device that pushes a rod up and down.

repel: to push back or away.

ACTUATORS

Besides a power source, robots have actuators. These are the muscles of the robot that let it perform work.

Some robots use hydraulic actuators. A hydraulic system uses fluids, such as water or oil, to create force. An electric motor or pump forces the fluid into a tube. This in turn pushes a piston. Hydraulic systems are very strong and are great for lifting heavy objects. Many industrial robots use hydraulics.

Pneumatic actuators work in a similar way, but they use air instead of fluid. These actuators aren't as strong as hydraulic actuators and are usually used for smaller jobs, such as enabling a robot to use its hands.

SOLENOIDS

Solenoids are another kind of actuator used in robotics. Solenoids are tube-like coils of wire with metal rods inside. When the coil is charged, it becomes electromagnetic, attracts the rod, and slides it farther into the coil. When the electricity is turned off, the metal rod is repelled, or pushed out along the coil. A solenoid can be used to push or pull an effector in a straight line. It might also be used to make a robot move its arm forward to push a button.

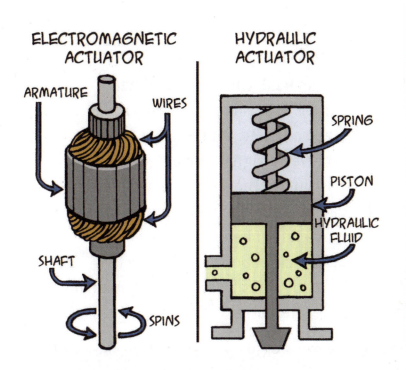

ELECTROMAGNETIC ACTUATOR

ARMATURE

WIRES

SHAFT

SPINS

HYDRAULIC ACTUATOR

SPRING

PISTON

HYDRAULIC FLUID

magnet: a piece of metal that attracts metal.

electromagnet: a magnet whose magnetism is turned on and off using electricity.

armature: the spinning part of a motor, made of tightly coiled wires.

shaft: the long, narrow part of an object.

wheg: a cross between a wheel and legs.

WORDS TO KNOW

The most common actuator used in robotics is a motor. If you looked inside a motor, you'd find magnets. Some of these magnets are permanent—they stay magnetic. Some of the magnets are electromagnets—these are turned on and off using electricity.

The armature, which is the part of the motor that turns, has a shaft, a long rod. The armature is covered in wires. When electricity flows through the wires, the armature becomes magnetic and is pushed and pulled by the permanent magnets around the armature. This movement causes the armature and shaft to spin.

Whegs are another way robots move around their environment. To create whegs, scientists at Case Western Reserve University studied how cockroaches move! **Take a look at this website.**

KEYWORD PROMPTS

Whegs wheel-leg robot

Many robots use a **servo**. This is a special kind of motor that can be programmed or controlled electronically. When the servo receives a signal, it changes the position of the shaft. This can be useful when the robot needs to move its limbs or turn its head. A biometric robot may have servos on each of its legs so they can move independently.

EFFECTORS

Anything that robots use to do their jobs or change their surroundings is called an effector. All kinds of things can be effectors.

A robotic lawn mower uses blades as its effector. The Telerob MV4, a firefighting robot, uses a fire extinguisher. The *Curiosity* rover has an arm for digging. Industrial robots might have screwdrivers or welding tools.

Robots also move in the space around them using effectors. The number of directions a robot can move is known as **degrees of freedom**. A robot might use **linear motion**, which is up and down or side to side, or it might use **rotational motion** to move in a circle.

DID YOU KNOW?

ASIMO has 34 degrees of freedom, not including its fingers.

Consider your own arm. Start at the shoulder. You can move your arm up and down as well as side to side. You can also rotate it in circles. This means your shoulder has three degrees of freedom.

Your elbow can go up and down, which is one degree of freedom. Your wrist can go up and down, side-to-side, and in circles. That's another three degrees of freedom. Altogether, your arm has seven degrees of freedom.

WHAT DO YOU CALL A ROBOT THAT LIKES TO READ?

A Readbot!

ROBOTS IN THE OPERATING ROOM!

Some effectors copy human movements. This can be useful when small or delicate movements are needed. The Da Vinci Surgical System does just that. A surgeon sits at a console with controls and a close-up view of the patient. In another part of the operating room, four robotic arms hold the tools, including scissors and scalpels. The surgeon's movements send signals to the tools, which can make smaller and more precise movements than a person can. The doctor and other surgical team members watch everything from monitors.

DID YOU KNOW?

In China in 2017, a robot performed the first dental surgery with no help from a human—although doctors were nearby. Would you feel comfortable having a robot work on your teeth?

Many robotic arms have a similar number of joints and degrees of freedom as we do. Some robots can lengthen their limbs as well. This is another degree of freedom. The more degrees of freedom a robot has, the more it can move.

But more degrees of freedom also means more challenges. It can take a long time to get all those parts to work together.

An important part of a robot's actuators is a robot's ability to sense its surroundings. How does it do that? We'll take a look in the next chapter!

 CONSIDER AND DISCUSS

It's time to consider and discuss: What kinds of jobs will robots do in the future?

DESIGN A SPACE ROBOT

Rovers are robotic vehicles that explore other planets, such as Mars. Here's a chance to design your own rover or space robot.

1 Decide which planet your robot will explore. Mars has a solid surface, but other planets, such as Jupiter, are made of gas and do not have solid surfaces. How will your robot move around?

2 Decide what task or tasks your robot will do. What kind of effectors will they need?

3 Consider how to power your robot. *Sojourner*, a Mars rover, used solar panels. Other robots use batteries or fuel.

TRY THIS!

Use items you find around your house to create a prototype of your space robot.

4 Start an engineering design worksheet to design your space robot. Sketch it in your journal.

MEET A SPACE ROBOT

Valkyrie is a 300-pound, 6-foot-tall humanoid built by NASA. Its official name is R5. Valkyrie runs on electricity or a battery and looks a little like the superhero Ironman! It has 44 degrees of freedom and can walk and step like a human. NASA hopes to use robots like Valkyrie to build shelters on Mars to prepare the way for astronauts.

PROJECT!

VIBRATING SOLAR ROBOT BUG

Some robots use vibration to move. Here's a fun project that uses recycled parts.

IMPORTANT: Ask an adult to help with the hot glue.

1 Pull the inside loop of each paperclip up into a **right angle**. Evenly space three of the paper clips along one side of the piece of cardboard and glue the short loops to the cardboard. Glue the rest of the paper clips along the other side of the cardboard in the same way. When the glue is dry, turn the cardboard over.

2 If you're scavenging a solar cell from an old garden light, remove any batteries that might be attached, but do NOT cut the two wires coming from the solar cell.

3 Glue the solar cell (but NOT the two wires) to the top of your cardboard bug.

4 If you're scavenging the vibrating motor from a battery-operated toothbrush, carefully remove it from the toothbrush case. With permission from an adult, you can search for videos of how to do this online. Each toothbrush is different. Do NOT cut the wires coming from it.

SUPPLIES

* 6 paper clips
* piece of cardboard a little bigger than the solar cell
* hot glue gun
* solar cell (can be recycled from solar garden lights or purchased at a hobby store)
* small vibrating motor (can be scavenged from a battery-operated toothbrush)
* electrical tape
* scissors
* two "robot eyes" (old resisters or LED lights, google eyes, small bolts)

WORDS TO KNOW

right angle: an angle that measures exactly 90 degrees, such as the corner of a square or rectangle.

5 Glue the motor to the bottom of the cardboard. It doesn't matter if it's touching the paper clips. Attach one of the motor wires to one of the wires from the solar cell by gently twisting them together. Use a small piece of electrical tape to secure them.

6 Twist together the other motor wire with the second solar cell wire and secure with electrical tape.

7 Add eyes to your robot bug by gluing them to the edge of the cardboard. Be careful not to attach them to the solar cell, or they'll block the sun's light.

8 Take your robot bug out into the bright sunlight. Set it down and watch it go! If your robot doesn't move, try charging the solar cell with a bright indoor light.

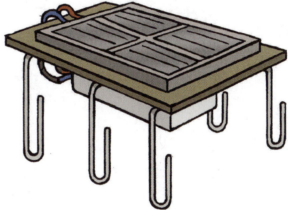

TRY THIS! Add jingle bells to your solar robot bug to turn it into a musical robot. Make sure the bells don't block the surface of your solar cell.

ROBOTIC HAND

Including the wrist, the human hand has 27 degrees of freedom. Robotic hands don't usually have as many degrees of freedom. See if you can figure out how many degrees of freedom this three-fingered robotic hand has.

SUPPLIES

* cardboard
* hot glue gun
* 4 to 5 drinking straws
* string or yarn
* Scotch tape (optional)

IMPORTANT: Ask an adult to help with the hot glue gun.

1 Cut out two pieces of cardboard that are 5 inches by 12 inches. Glue them together to form one strong base.

2 Cut more cardboard into three pieces that are 1 inch by 6 inches and cut another piece that is 1 inch by 4 inches. These will be your robot's fingers and thumb. Glue the three taller fingers to one end of the base. Glue the thumb at the corner of the base at an angle, like a real thumb.

3 Make creases in the fingers to make three joints. Crease the thumb to make two joints. Each of the bottom joints should be where the fingers attach to the base.

4 Cut the straws so that you have 12 pieces that are 1-inch long for the fingers. Cut four pieces that are three-quarters of an inch long for the thumb. Use the hot glue gun to attach a piece of straw in between each joint and at the bottom of each finger. Do the same for the thumb using the smaller pieces of straws.

5 Starting at the top of each finger, thread a piece of string through the straws, leaving about 6 inches of string at the top of the straw. At the bottom of the string, tie a loop.

6 Use a piece of cardboard to make a handle. Lay your hand palm up on the base to see where to position the handle. You want the handle to fit just over your fingers. Once you've found a good spot, glue the handle to the base.

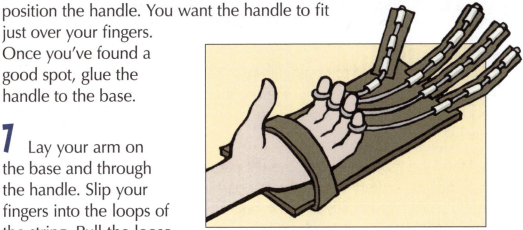

7 Lay your arm on the base and through the handle. Slip your fingers into the loops of the string. Pull the loose piece of string at the top of the robot finger to take up the slack. You'll have to experiment with how long to make the strings. You want the string to be long enough so the loop fits around the tip of your finger, but short enough so it can pull the robot finger down.

8 Once you get a good length for each string, make a knot at each top straw. You can put a dab of hot glue on the straw to help keep the string in place. To operate your robotic hand, slip your palm under the handle and use your own fingertips to pull the strings!

> **CONSIDER THIS!** How many degrees of freedom does the robotic hand have?

MAKE A SOLENOID

A solenoid uses electromagnetism to push or pull a rod. See how a solenoid works.

> **IMPORTANT:** You will need an adult to help you with this project.

1 Have an adult use the utility knife to cut off the bottom part of the syringe, where the medicine comes out.

2 Stand the tube up so that the flat part is on top and hold it in place. Lay the battery across the flat part to form a T. Use the electrical tape to attach the battery to the syringe.

3 Leaving about 6 inches of wire free at the end, begin wrapping the wire around the syringe about an inch from the bottom. Wrap the wire up the tube in tight rows to make a coil around 1 inch tall.

4 Begin wrapping the wire down the tube over the previous coil. When you get to the bottom, wrap the wire back up the previous layers. Keep wrapping the wire in tight rows, up and down, until you have about 6 inches of wire left on the end. This step might take a while. You'll have a LOT of coils!

5 Have an adult strip the ends of the wires so you have about one-half inch of bare wire showing. Tape one of these pieces of bare wire to one end of the battery. It doesn't matter which end of the battery you choose.

6 Hold the syringe upright about 1 inch from your table. Slip the nail into the tube until the flat end of the nail hangs out of the tube. It can rest on the table.

7 To turn on your electromagnet, touch the loose wire to the other end of the battery. The nail will be pulled into the tube. When you pull the wire away from the battery, the nail will be pushed out. If the nail doesn't move, try using sandpaper to rough it up a bit. Sometimes, nails have paint or special coatings on them that might prevent them from being magnetic. Also, check to see if the wire is still attached to the battery because it can come loose under the tape.

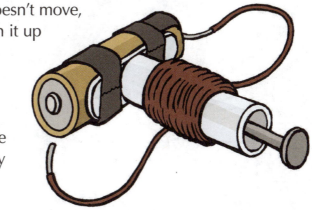

TRY THIS! List other things around your house that use electromagnetism. Here's a few to get you started: doorbells, speakers, telephones.

WANT TOAST? YOU NEED A SOLENOID!

After you put your bread in a toaster, you push down a lever. When you do, a tiny metal spring is compressed (pushed down). After the bread is toasted, a solenoid releases a latch that's holding the spring. The spring expands and up pops your toast.

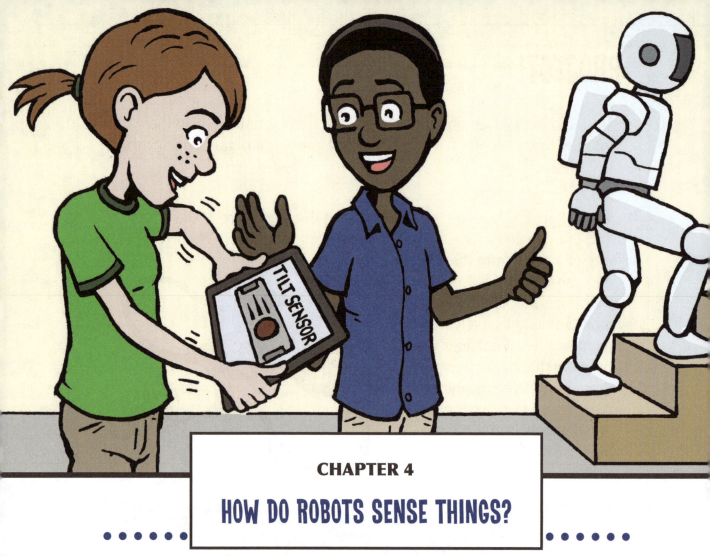

CHAPTER 4

HOW DO ROBOTS SENSE THINGS?

Humans have five senses. We can see, hear, touch, taste, and smell. We use these senses to take in information about the world around us. We rely on our senses to keep us safe and active.

Robots can take in information about their environments, too. They gather information using a variety of sensors. Many of these sensors are similar to our own senses. But some are different, allowing robots to do things humans can't.

 INVESTIGATE!

What senses do humans and robots have in common?

HOW DO ROBOTS SEE?

Our eyes detect light waves and send signals to our brains, which figure out what we're seeing. Robots don't have eyes, but many of them have cameras that allow them to "see." They can also send pictures back to the human who is operating the robot.

For example, Snakebot is a 3-foot-long robot that looks and moves like a snake and has a seeing-eye camera. Because it is small and can wiggle into cramped spaces, Snakebot can be used in search-and-rescue missions.

light waves: waves made from magnetic and electric fields moving back and forth.

chemical: the pure form of a substance. Some chemicals can be combined or broken up to create new chemicals.

WORDS TO KNOW

DID YOU KNOW?

Owlstone Medical, a company in Cambridge, England, is testing a chemical sensor to analyze a patient's breath and detect diseases such as cancer. Smell and taste are challenging for roboticists because so many chemicals make up odors and tastes.

We can see sunlight and other types of light. But robots can also see light rays that are invisible to humans. Ultraviolet (UV) light rays are part of the energy that comes from the sun. These are rays that can give you a sunburn. Robots can sense UV light in order to detect fires.

A SCORPION UNDER UV LIGHT. THERE ARE A LOT OF THINGS HUMANS MISS BECAUSE WE CAN'T SEE UV LIGHT. CREDIT: JERRY KIRKHART (CC BY 2.0)

Infrared (IR) is another type of light that is invisible to humans. But even though we can't see it, we can feel IR light as heat.

Have you ever seen or used night-vision goggles? These goggles allow people to see at night by detecting the IR waves that objects and living creatures give off. An IR sensor can be helpful when rescue robots are looking for missing people.

Robots also use a combination of IR sensors and emitters to determine the distances to objects. For example, if you don't want the Roomba to go into a certain room, you can set up an emitter. The emitter sends out a beam of light that bounces off the Roomba and back to an IR sensor. This tells the vacuum cleaner not to go past that point.

> infrared (IR): a type of light with a longer wavelength than visible light, which can also be felt as heat.
>
> emitter: a device that sends out a light or sound wave or other signal.
>
> ## WORDS TO KNOW

DISASTER CITY

People who help victims of natural disasters need to practice their search-and-rescue skills. That's where Disaster City comes in. Disaster City is a 52-acre fake city in College Station, Texas. The "city" has collapsed buildings, damaged businesses and houses, and piles of rubble where rescue crews can practice finding and helping people. Sometimes, this means using search robots to get into small or especially dangerous areas. Training in realistic environments such as these help roboticists develop new and better robots.

WORDS TO KNOW

sonar: a way to detect objects by bouncing sound waves off them and measuring how long it takes to detect an echo.

echo: sound waves that bounce off a distant object and reflect back to the place they started.

radar: a device that detects objects by bouncing radio waves off them and measuring how long it takes for the waves to return.

lidar: a device that measures distance by shining a laser or other light at an object and measuring the time it takes for the light to return.

HEAR THAT?

Robots also use a form of hearing to sense the world around them. Some animals, including whales and bats, use sonar to find things in the ocean or at night. They bounce sound waves off an object and see how long it takes for those sound waves to bounce back—like an echo. Radar is similar, except it uses radio waves, and lidar uses laser lights. Robots use all of these.

SHREW-D

Robots can also figure out how close they are to something by using touch-sensitive feelers. Bristol Robotics Laboratory's Shrewbot is one such robot. Like the way cats and rats use their whiskers, Shrewbot uses long feelers made of thin pieces of wire to gather information about its surroundings. Someday, Shrewbot's feelers might make it able to explore dark spaces or even other planets.

PS You can see Shrewbot in a video and study a diagram of its body at this website.

KEYWORD PROMPTS

Popsci Shrewbot

Switches are another way robots can tell if something is in their way. Switches are controls that open and close a circuit. We use switches every time we turn on a light or a computer.

Bumper sensors are sensors that use tiny switches. When a robot with a bumper sensor runs into an object, the switch is turned on or off. This sends a signal for the robot to change direction or stop.

bumper sensor: a device that uses tiny switches that turn on and off when a robot bumps into something.

WORDS ⊙ KNOW

·· DID YOU KNOW? ·········

Through pressure sensors, robots can detect temperature and texture and figure out how much pressure is needed to hold an object.

ROBOTICS!

A BALANCING ACT

In order to walk, robots need a sense of balance. Getting a robot to balance takes a lot of work. Balance requires many movements and constant adjustments on the robot's part. Two simple types of sensors that can help robots balance are **tilt sensors** and **accelerometers**.

A tilt sensor, also called a tilt switch or a rolling ball sensor, is a device made up of a tube with a small, metal ball inside. At one end of the tube are two wires.

When the robot leans or extends one of its limbs, the ball begins to roll. If it moves too far, the metal ball connects with the wires and sends the robot a signal to adjust its position.

WHAT DO GET WHEN YOU CROSS A ROBOT AND A SKUNK?

R-2-P-U

Watch the robot Atlas jog, jump, and flip! Accelerometers allow robots such as Boston Dynamic's Atlas to jog and even pull off amazing backflips!

KEYWORD PROMPTS

Boston Dynamics Atlas

NOW HEAR THIS!

Because humans have two ears and our ears are complex organs, we usually do a pretty good job of figuring out where a sound came from. But robots have a tougher time. The microphones robots use as their ears take in every sound. Humans, on the other hand, can tune out unimportant background noise. But researchers are working to improve this. HEARBO is a robot developed at Honda Research Institute in Japan. Using eight microphones, HEARBO can locate sound from four different sources at the same time. In the future, robots might locate sounds better than humans!

An accelerometer is an instrument that measures changes in speed. It does this by detecting very small movements of a weight. Let's say a walking robot trips over an obstacle and begins falling. As the robot leans over, the weight in its accelerometer shifts and changes speed. This change sends an electrical signal that tells the robot to respond.

Accelerometers tell robots if they have suddenly run into something, are tilting, or have left the ground. They are also what make it possible for you to turn a smartphone and rotate what you're seeing!

Now, it's time to put it all together! In the next chapter, we'll learn how robots process all the information they gather through their sensors!

? CONSIDER AND DISCUSS

It's time to consider and discuss: What senses do humans and robots have in common?

PROJECT!

GLOWING IN THE DARK

UV radiation is what causes things to glow under "black light" bulbs. You can see for yourself what is emitting UV rays!

1 Screw the black light bulb into a lamp that's in a dark room. Turn it on.

2 Hold the variety of objects under the light. Make the following observations.

- Which ones glow?

- Do some of the objects glow more brightly? Which ones?

- Which colors seem to glow best?

3 Record your observations in your journal. Can you find any patterns to your observations?

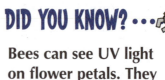

DID YOU KNOW?

Bees can see UV light on flower petals. They use it to find pollen.

TRY THIS! Try out unusual objects such as petroleum jelly, Mountain Dew, and bananas with spots. If you find any dead beetles or other insects, try looking at those. Make sure to wash your hands afterwards! How about plants or flowers? What are those living things hiding?

SUPPLIES

- ✳ a black light (found where light bulbs are sold)
- ✳ journal and pencil
- ✳ a variety of objects to test

PROJECT!

BECOME A SHREWBOT

Experience how animals and robots use touch-sensitive feelers to explore their environments.

1 Twist the end of a pipe cleaner around the tip of one of your fingers. The pipe cleaner should be snug but not too tight. You can have the pipe cleaners going straight up from your fingers, **vertically**, or bend them so they're coming off your fingers **horizontally**.

2 Twist pipe cleaners around the rest of your fingers and thumbs in the same way. You might need your friend to help.

3 Close your eyes or use a blindfold and walk around the room while your friend guides you. Use your "feelers" to see how close you are to obstacles. Can you feel the vibrations travel down the pipe cleaners when you brush up against something?

TRY THIS! Give your friend a chance to try out the pipe cleaners. Can you make it from room to room?

WORDS ⊕ KNOW

vertical: straight up and down.

horizontal: straight across from side to side.

SUPPLIES

* 10 pipe cleaners (new and straight work best)
* a friend
* blindfold (optional)

LOCATE SOUNDS

**Humans can locate sounds better than robots. But
how good are you at telling which direction a sound is coming from?**

1 Have one person, person #1, sit in the middle of a room, wearing the headphones and the blindfold. Person #2 will be the "recorder" and stay with the blindfolded person to help collect data and tell the person when to remove the headphones.

2 Have person #3 move around the room. Once they stop, the recorder (person #2) should tap person #1 to let them know it's time to remove the headphones.

3 Have person #3 make a sound, such as finger snapping or a clap or ringing a bell. The blindfolded person must guess where the sound came from. The recorder writes down this information.

4 Have person #1 put the headphones back on and person #3 repeat the process of moving around and making sounds several times, while person #2 records the blindfolded person's guess each time.

5 Have each person switch places until everyone has had a turn. What were the results? Could the blindfolded person figure out where the sounds were coming from?

TRY THIS! Have the blindfolded person cover one ear when the sound is made. Or add music or other background noise to the room. What difference do these things make to someone's ability to locate the sound?

PROJECT!

MAKE AN ACCELEROMETER

This simple accelerometer uses a cork as a weight. It'll give you a basic idea of how accelerometers work.

SUPPLIES

* cork
* small screw
* string
* tape
* jar with lid
* water

1 Carefully twist the screw into the middle of one end of the cork. For a cork recycled from a bottle, use the undamaged end.

2 Cut a piece of string that is a little longer than the jar is tall. Tie one end of the string to the top of the screw. Make a small knot at the other end of the string and tape it to the middle of the bottom of the jar lid.

3 Fill the jar with water. Place the cork and string into the water and screw on the jar lid so it's tightly closed. Flip the jar over. The cork should be floating approximately in the middle of the jar. If it's not, flip the jar right side up, take off the lid and adjust the string length as needed. This is your accelerometer.

4 Set your accelerometer on the table and slide it around at various speeds. Be careful not to push it off the table. What does the cork do?

WHAT'S HAPPENING? If you move the jar to the right, the cork leans to the right. If you move it to the left, the cork leans left. The **densities** of the cork and water are different. Density affects an object's **inertia**—the tendency of an object at rest to stay at rest. Because of its greater density, the water wants to move, but the cork wants to stay where it is. The water, however, pushes the cork in the direction it's going. Robots use accelerometers to know where they are in space.

WORDS TO KNOW

density: a measure of how closely packed items are.

inertia: the tendency of an object at rest to do nothing until an outside force acts on it.

69

PROJECT!

MAKE A MINI FLASHLIGHT

We use pressure sensors all the time. Here's a fun and easy way to make your own pressure sensor to create a mini flashlight.

1 Squash your toilet paper roll down so it makes a 2½-by-4-inch rectangle. Use the scissors to cut the fold along the right side and open the tube flat.

2 Cut two pieces of foil that are 2 inches by 4 inches long. Glue one strip of foil to the left side of the flattened toilet paper roll and the second strip to the right side of the roll. Make sure that all the foil is glued down flat.

3 Cut two 2-by-2-inch pieces of cardboard. Carefully cut an inner square inside each piece that's big enough for the battery to fit inside. Glue the two squares together. If you are using a thick piece of cardboard, you may need only one square. The cardboard needs to be a little thicker than the battery.

4 Glue the cardboard window in the middle of the right side of the rectangle.

SUPPLIES

* toilet paper roll
* scissors
* tin foil
* glue
* cardboard
* small round battery
* LED light bulb with two metal legs
* electrical tape
* markers (optional)

PROJECT!

5 Find the positive and negative sides of the battery. The positive side has a + on it. Turn the battery over to the negative (-) side and carefully spread glue along the edge of the battery. Glue it inside the cardboard window so the positive (+) side is facing up.

6 Lay the LED light on the top edge of the left side of the rectangle. The LED has two wires coming from it and one is longer than the other. Tape the long wire to the foil. The bulb should hang off the edge of the cardboard.

7 Put a little piece of tape under the short wire so that the sticky part of the tape is facing out. Next, carefully fold the left side of the rectangle over the right side. Gently press the wire and tape it down.

8 Test your mini flashlight by pressing in the middle of the card. When the foil is touching the battery, the LED should light up. If it doesn't, check to see if the LED wires are taped down and that you are pressing hard enough.

TRY THIS! Once your flashlight lights up, you can tape the edges and decorate the outside of it.

CHAPTER 5

HOW DO ROBOTS THINK?

• •

Robots are able to gather lots of information from their environments, and they can put that information to good use. But how? What's going on inside a robot that allows it to think?

• •

The information that robots take in from their sensors is called input. The action or response of a robot to this information is called output. Between input and output is when processing happens. Robots don't have brains like we do, but they do have ways to process information. A robot's brain is its microprocessor.

? **INVESTIGATE!**

Will robots be smarter than humans someday?

⋯ DID YOU KNOW? ⋯⋯⋯

We use microprocessors all the time. Laptops, tablets, and smartphones all have them!

input: a signal or information that is put into a machine or robot.

output: the response of a robot to the input it receives from its sensors.

microprocessor: a small electronic chip that manages information and controls what a computer does.

software: the programs and other operating information used by a computer.

WORDS TO KNOW

A microprocessor is a collection of computer chips that can deal with a lot of information in a very short amount of time. Some of these are very small. IBM has developed a prototype of a computer chip that is smaller than the width of a human hair! But many computer chips are about the size of a postage stamp.

When a robot takes in information from its sensors, it's not really thinking about what to do next. Humans create software that controls the steps the microprocessor—and therefore the robot—carries out.

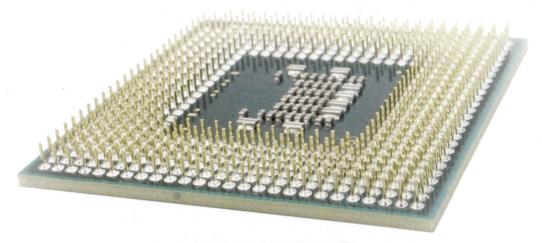

NOT ACTUAL SIZE! MOST COMPUTER CHIPS ARE VERY TINY.

FLOWCHARTS

Breaking up a job into smaller, simpler steps makes big jobs easier to do. The same is true for writing software or code. Programmers usually begin by breaking down the task the computer needs to perform into smaller steps. A **flowchart** is a good way to do this.

Flowcharts use YES and NO questions. Let's say you want to make a sandwich. The flowchart for the process might look like this. Flowcharts for **computer programs** are usually much more complicated!

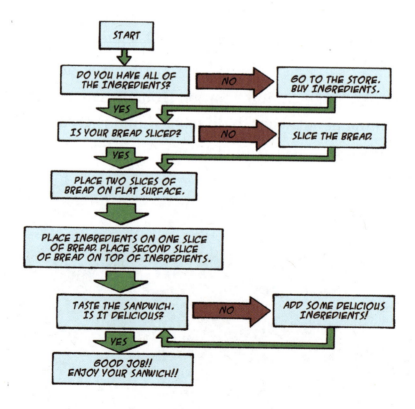

computer science: the study of computers and how they work.

artificial intelligence: also known as AI, the intelligence of a computer, program, or machine.

WORDS ⊙ KNOW

HOW SMART ARE ROBOTS?

We can program robots and other machines to solve problems and do jobs for us. Robots can do amazing things, as we've seen in this book. But they can't think or make decisions all on their own—yet. The branch of computer science that deals with computers' ability to imitate human intelligence is called artificial intelligence (AI).

Robots might sometimes look like us, but they don't think like us. Perhaps getting them to *act* more like us will help them think like humans. In 1996, an IBM computer called Deep Blue beat a chess champion. And in 2011, IBM's Watson played and beat two champions of the trivia game show *Jeopardy!* Programmers had to supply Watson with all the data it needed and teach Watson to understand the clues to the questions.

Watson did well because it learned from its mistakes. Teaching machines how to learn is something scientists are working on.

Some people find this scary. What if robots rise up and take over the world? Fortunately, that's not likely to happen. And having robots that are smarter than us has advantages.

For example, in 2016, a computer program called AlphaGo played 18-time world champion Go player Lee Sedol (1983–). Go is a very complicated game of strategy that involves moving stones on a playing board. Because it could calculate a large variety of moves, AlphaGo pushed our human understanding of the game. AlphaGo thought of moves even world-class players hadn't imagined. Humans learned from the machine!

ON A GO BOARD, THE FIRST PLAYER HAS 360 OPTIONS OF WHERE TO MOVE. IT'S COMPLEX!

ALMOST HUMAN?

Can machines be so human-like that they pass for a person? In 1950, computer scientist Alan Turing (1912–1954) came up with a test, now called the Turing test, to find out. In the Turing test, you use a keyboard and screen to see if you can tell if you're communicating with a computer or a human.

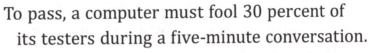

WHY DID THE ROBOT CROSS THE ROAD?

Its microprocessor told it to!

To pass, a computer must fool 30 percent of its testers during a five-minute conversation. No computer had passed the Turing test until 2014, when a computer program pretending to be a 13-year-old boy fooled 33 percent of the testers.

Computers can also make sure you're a human through the CAPTCHA (which stands for completely automated public Turing test to tell computers and humans apart) test. You've probably taken a CAPTCHA test if a website has asked you to look at distorted words or a series of numbers and type what you see inside a box.

Robots have many uses in our world, and they're getting more and more advanced as scientists develop new hardware and software. Now that you know more about them, you can spot the robots that share your world, even when they aren't humanoids. Maybe you'll be the person to come up with a new, more advanced kind of artificial intelligence!

? CONSIDER AND DISCUSS

It's time to consider and discuss: Will robots be smarter than humans someday?

TEACH A ROBOT

Some people worry that robots will take over all the jobs that humans do. But while robots are doing more jobs, they also create jobs. One such robot is Sawyer, a friendly looking, one-armed robot from Rethink Robotics that does dangerous or boring jobs in factories. Robots such as this are often called cobots because they work alongside humans, like co-workers. Someone must maintain and train Sawyer how to complete its tasks by physically moving its arm. Do you think you could be a robot trainer? For this experiment, you just need a friend.

1 Decide on a task with your friend. For example, pouring a glass of milk. Decide who will be the robot and who will be the robot trainer. Make sure the robot is okay with being touched by the trainer.

2 Without talking to the robot, have the trainer show the robot how to pour a glass of milk by physically moving the robot's arms, hands, and fingers.

3 How did the training go? Was it harder or easier than you thought it would be?

TRY THIS! Switch places and try the experiment again doing a different task.

WORDS to **KNOW**

cobot: an industrial robot that works alongside humans.

PROJECT!

BUILD YOUR OWN BATTLING ROBOT

Can you build your own battling robot that can knock over a stack of blocks?

1 Make a new body for the remote-controlled car using an old box or container. Cut a hole in the container so the car's antenna can poke through and receive your signals.

2 Decorate the outside of your battling robot using paint, pipe cleaners, and other craft supplies. Use tape or glue to attach the new body over the car.

3 Attach various effectors, such as popsicle sticks or straws, to the front of the new body.

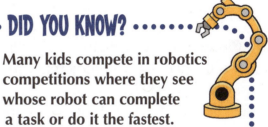

• • • DID YOU KNOW? • • • • • • • •

Many kids compete in robotics competitions where they see whose robot can complete a task or do it the fastest.

4 Set up some blocks as an obstacle and test your battling robot by driving it into the blocks. Did it knock the block tower over? If not, try another effector.

> **TRY THIS!** Invite a friend to build their own battling robot. Set up an obstacle course and race your robot against theirs through the course.

SUPPLIES

* ✳ remote-controlled car that works
* ✳ old box, plastic container, or 2-liter bottle
* ✳ scissors
* ✳ tape or glue
* ✳ paint, pipe cleaners, and other craft supplies
* ✳ effectors such as popsicle sticks or straws
* ✳ blocks

PROJECT!

WRITE "CODE" TO MAKE A SANDWICH

Programmers must break tasks down into simple steps when they write code for computers. This can be harder than it sounds! Try this experiment to test your skills.

1 Write step-by-step instructions to make a peanut butter and jelly sandwich and put it on a plate or napkin. Look over your steps. Do you think your friend will be able to make a sandwich successfully? Make a hypothesis.

2 Read your directions out loud to your friend and have them follow the steps exactly.

3 Observe what happens and record the results in your journal. How did it go? Did you remember to write instructions to open the jar of peanut butter? Did you remember to tell your partner how many pieces of bread to use? Was your hypothesis correct?

4 If your directions were confusing, rewrite them and do the experiment again.

TRY THIS! Have your friend write step-by-step instructions for another task, perhaps tying a shoe. Try following the directions to perform the task.

SUPPLIES

✳ journal
✳ pen or pencil

DESIGN A TURING TEST

Can you tell if you're talking to a machine or a real person? Design your own Turing test to find out.

1 Think about the ways robots and other machines are different from humans. For example, humans have emotions and a sense of humor. Humans are alive and machines are not.

2 Keeping these differences in mind, brainstorm questions you could ask that might give you a clue whether you are talking to a real person or a machine. Write them in your journal.

Some ideas to get you started include the following.

• How do turtles talk to each other? Answer: With shell phones. (This question would see if the person/machine understands puns.)

• I feel blue. What does that mean? (This question might see if the person/machine understands how words can be used in different ways.)

• Can you tell me what 20,756 x 5,188 is? (A machine would probably be able to do this math problem quicker than a human.)

• Can you make up a story? (This question might see if the person/machine is creative.)

TRY THIS! There are many virtual assistant devices available today, including Amazon Alexa, Google Assistant, and Apple Siri. Ask one your questions and see how it responds.

ROBOT GLOSSARY SCAVENGER HUNT

We've learned a lot of words in this book. Here's something fun you can do with them!

1 Use the glossary to answer these questions.

- What is a cobot?

- An _____ lets a robot affect things in the outside world.
  An _____ is a piece of equipment that makes robots move.

- What is a humanoid?

- NASA is an acronym for what?

- A signal or information that is put into a machine or robot is called _____.

- A microscopic robot is called a _____.

- Find two examples of a robot sensor.

- Would you like to have a bionic body part?

- What is the Uncanny Valley?

- A group of identical robots designed to work together as a team is called a _____.

- Degrees of _____ refers to the number of directions in which a robot effector or other part can move.

- A _____ is someone who studies robotics.

TRY THIS! Come up with your own scavenger hunt questions and let a friend or family member play.

3-D printing: the process of making a three-dimensional object using various materials.

accelerometer: an electronic device that measures acceleration, which is the change in speed or direction of an object.

acronym: a word or name formed using the first letters of other words.

actuator: a piece of equipment that makes a robot move.

agile: able to move quickly and with ease.

algorithm: a set of steps that are followed to solve a mathematical problem or to complete a computer process.

android: a robot with a human appearance.

animatronic: making a puppet or other lifelike figure move on its own with electronics.

armature: the spinning part of a motor, made of tightly coiled wires.

artificial intelligence: also known as AI, the intelligence of a computer, program, or machine.

automata: machines that can move by themselves. Singular is automaton.

battery: a device that produces an electric current using chemicals.

BCE: put after a date, BCE stands for Before Common Era and counts down to zero. CE stands for Common Era and counts up from zero. These non-religious terms correspond to BC and AD. This book was printed in 2019 CE.

biometric: looking or behaving like something from nature, especially animals.

bionic: a mechanical or computer-driven device that replaces or improves the normal ability of a body part.

bumper sensor: a device that uses tiny switches that turn on and off when a robot bumps into something.

cancer cell: a normal cell in the body that changes and grows out of control.

chemical: the pure form of a substance. Some chemicals can be combined or broken up to create new chemicals.

cobot: an industrial robot that works alongside humans.

colleague: a person you work with.

compressed air: air that is under more pressure than the outside air.

computer program: a set of step-by-step instructions that tells a computer what to do.

computer science: the study of computers and how they work.

cyborg: a human or animal that is part robot.

data: information gathered from tests or experiments.

degrees of freedom: the number of directions in which a robot effector or other part can move.

density: a measure of how closely packed items are.

digital: using numbers to express information.

disarm: to make something harmless.

echo: sound waves that bounce off a distant object and reflect back to the place they started.

effector: a device that lets a robot affect things in the outside world, such as a gripper, tool, or laser beam.

electrical circuit: the pathway electricity follows.

electromagnet: a magnet whose magnetism is turned on and off using electricity.

emitter: a device that sends out a light or sound wave or other signal.

emotion: a strong feeling about something or somebody.

engineer: a person who uses science, math, and creativity to design and build things.

engineering: the use of science, math, and creativity in the design and construction of things.

enhance: to make greater.

environment: physical surroundings.

exoskeleton: a skeleton on the outside of a body.

flowchart: a diagram that shows all the possible options and results.

force: a push or pull applied to an object.

gears: wheels with interlocking teeth that transfer motion from one part of a machine to another.

germs: microscopic organisms that can cause harm. An organism is a living thing.

GPS: Global Positioning System, a device that determines its location on Earth using signals sent from different satellites in space.

horizontal: straight across from side to side.

humanoid: looking like a human being.

hydraulic: describes a system that pushes and pulls objects using tubes filled with fluid.

industrial robot: a robot that works in a factory or a manufacturing setting.

inertia: the tendency of an object at rest to do nothing until an outside force acts on it.

inflection: a rise or fall in the sound of a person's voice.

infrared (IR): a type of light with a longer wavelength than visible light, which can also be felt as heat.

input: a signal or information that is put into a machine or robot.

International Space Station: a massive space station orbiting Earth where astronauts live, conduct experiments, and study space.

intrigue: to arouse the curiosity or interest of someone.

lidar: a device that measures distance by shining a laser or other light at an object and measuring the time it takes for the light to return.

light waves: waves made from magnetic and electric fields moving back and forth.

linear motion: movement in a straight line.

liquefy: to turn into a liquid.

magnet: a piece of metal that attracts metal.

manipulate: to handle, use, or control an object in a skillful way.

mechanical: done by machine, not by a person.

microprocessor: a small electronic chip that manages information and controls what a computer does.

microscopic: something so small it can be seen only using a microscope.

mimic: to copy something.

modern: relating to the present time, a style that is new or different, or based on the newest information or technology.

nanobot: a microscopic robot.

NASA: National Aeronautics and Space Administration, the U.S. organization in charge of space exploration.

natural disaster: a natural event, such as a fire or flood, that causes great damage.

nuclear power: power produced by splitting atoms, the tiniest pieces of matter.

output: the response of a robot to the input it receives from its sensors.

paralyzed: unable to move.

piston: a short, solid piece of metal that moves up and down inside a cylinder to create motion.

pneumatic: describes a system that pushes and pulls objects using tubes filled with air or other gases.

precise: exact or detailed.

programmer: a person who writes computer programs. Also called a coder.

prototype: a working model or mock-up that allows engineers to test their solution.

pulley: a rope on a wheel used to lift things.

punch card: a card with holes punched in it that gives directions to a machine or computer.

radar: a device that detects objects by bouncing radio waves off them and measuring how long it takes for the waves to return.

radio wave: a type of invisible wave used to transmit radio and television signals. Radio waves are also used for navigation.

repel: to push back or away.

right angle: an angle that measures exactly 90 degrees, such as the corner of a square or rectangle.

robot: a machine that can move and do tasks without help from a human.

roboticist: a scientist who studies robotics.

robotics: the science of designing, building, controlling, and operating robots.

rotational motion: movement around the center of something.

rover: a vehicle used to explore the surface of a planet or a moon.

science fiction: a story about contact with other worlds and imaginary science and technology.

scripted: written ahead of time.

sensor: something that allows a robot to see or sense its environment.

servo: a motor that can be controlled electronically.

shaft: the long, narrow part of an object.

silicone: a flexible, rubber-like plastic.

software: the programs and other operating information used by a computer.

solar cell: a device that converts light energy into electricity.

solar power: energy from the sun converted to electricity.

solenoid: an electromagnetic device that pushes a rod up and down.

sonar: a way to detect objects by bouncing sound waves off them and measuring how long it takes to detect an echo.

swarm: a group of identical robots designed to work together as a team.

technology: the tools, methods, and systems used to solve a problem or do work.

terrain: land or ground and all its physical features, such as hills, rocks, and water.

terrestrial body: a planet or moon that has a solid surface.

tilt sensor: a device that uses a metal ball inside a tube to turn on or off a switch when the tube is titled.

torso: the human body except the head, arms, and legs.

transistor: a small device that acts as an on/off switch to control the flow of electricity in a computer.

tread: a travel system that uses a continuous band of tracks.

ultraviolet (UV): a type of light with shorter wavelengths than visible light. Also called black light.

Uncanny Valley: the point at which a robot looks almost real and becomes strange and frightening.

vacuum tube: an electronic component that looks like a light bulb. It was used as an on/off switch in early computers and other appliances.

vertical: straight up and down.

voice recognition: the ability of a machine to recognize and respond to a human voice.

wheg: a cross between a wheel and legs.

zashiki karakuri: early Japanese automata that could serve tea.

METRIC CONVERSIONS

Use this chart to find the metric equivalents to the English measurements in this book. If you need to know a half measurement, divide by two. If you need to know twice the measurement, multiply by two. How do you find a quarter measurement? How do you find three times the measurement?

English	Metric
1 inch	2.5 centimeters
1 foot	30.5 centimeters
1 yard	0.9 meter
1 mile	1.6 kilometers
1 pound	0.5 kilogram
1 teaspoon	5 milliliters
1 tablespoon	15 milliliters
1 cup	237 milliliters

BOOKS

Becker, Helaine. *Zoobots: Wild Robots Inspired by Real Animals*. Kids Can Press, 2014.

Bridgman, Roger. *Robot*. DK Eyewitness Books, 2004.

Chow-Miller, Ian. *How Robots Work*. Everyday Stem, 2018.

DK Findout: *Robots!* Penguin Random House, 2018.

McComb, Gordon. *Building Your Own Robots*. John Wiley and Sons, 2016.

Steward, Melissa. *Robots*. National Geographic Children's Books, 2014.

Swanson, Jennifer. *Everything Robotics*. National Geographic Children's Books, 2016.

WEBSITES

Simple Bots Instructables:
instructables.com/id/Simple-Bots

Science Kids Robots:
sciencekids.co.nz/robots.html

Robot Hall of Fame: robothalloffame.org

NASA: What is Robotics?
nasa.gov/audience/forstudents/k-4/stories/nasa-knows/
what_is_robotics_k4.html

Digital.com: digital.com/blog/robotics-resources

MUSEUMS

These Smithsonian museums (all in Washington, DC) use robot guides:
Hirshhorn Museum and Sculpture Garden
National Museum of African American Museum of History and Culture
The Smithsonian Castle
Smithsonian Environmental Research Center

Carnegie Science Center: Robot Hall of Fame in Pittsburg, Pennsylvania

Robot Science Museum in Seoul, South Korea (opening in 2022)

The Mansfield Memorial Museum
(permanent home of Electro, the Westinghouse robot) in Mansfield, Ohio

ESSENTIAL QUESTIONS

Introduction: How many robots can you find in your home right now? Do you think that number will change in the future?

Chapter 1: Why are people fascinated by robots?

Chapter 2: Why do robots often look like humans or animals?

Chapter 3: What kinds of jobs will robots do in the future?

Chapter 4: What senses do humans and robots have in common?

Chapter 5: Will robots be smarter than humans someday?

QR CODE GLOSSARY

Page 5: youtube.com/watch?v=R7-Hd3I9vjI

Page 12: leonardodavincisinventions.com/mechanical-inventions/leonardo-da-vincis-car

Page 15: youtube.com/watch?v=lLULRlmXkKo

Page 16: youtube.com/watch?v=xyj6N-i6asQ

Page 26: youtube.com/watch?v=oJq5PQZHU-I

Page 29: youtube.com/watch?v=LjbyxekEo6s

Page 30: youtube.com/watch?v=8KRZX5KL4fA

Page 39: robonaut.jsc.nasa.gov/r2/pages/iss-mission.html

Page 47: youtube.com/watch?v=F4GF2UFhv8Y

Page 62: popsci.com/technology/article/2013-07/blind-robot-navigates-touch-blueprint

Page 64: bostondynamics.com/atlas